BLOOD FROM THIS ALTAR

Aaron Zufelt

Copyright © 2021 Aaron Zufelt

All rights reserved

The characters and events portrayed in this book are fictitious. Any similarity to real persons, living or dead, is coincidental and not intended by the author.

No part of this book may be reproduced, or stored in a retrieval system, or transmitted in any form or by any means, electronic, mechanical, photocopying, recording, or otherwise, without express written permission of the publisher.

ISBN-13: 9798498760445

Cover design by: AZ
Library of Congress Control Number: 2018675309
Printed in the United States of America

To my incredibly wonderful children. May their lives always be full of joy and wonder, and when it is not, may they find the courage to strive and find it. To my soulmate, don't stop looking for me.

Herein is the evil of ignorance; he who is neither good nor wise is nevertheless satisfied with himself.

PLATO

CONTENTS

Title Page
Copyright
Dedication
Epigraph
Introduction
to the reader...

The search	1
Clouds Upon the Glen	2
Tamer of the universe	5
Luna	7
Worn Old Men	8
Ebb	9
Larking	10
Woven	11
Wistful	12
Unopened Books	13
Tomorrow	14
The Fallen	15
Gilded Lilies	16
Of Devils And Gods	17
Lost Virtue	18
Of Tides and Towers	19
Summer	20
Eyes	21

Her Face	22
My Ancient Pictographs	23
A Child Cries (Oklahoma Bombing)	24
Added Upon	25
Sleep Falls on the Mountain	26
Sum of Life	27
Life's Abacus	28
Life…	29
Larking	30
From the Dead New Life	31
Tangled Leaves	32
The Weight of Winters	33
Raindrop On The Back Porch Railing	35
Forest Pine: Part One	36
Forest Pine: Part Two	38
Glimpses of Bull Trout Lake	40
In The Middle	41
Thank You Child	44
Soul Forge	45
Some Reason More	46
Restless the Night	47
The Pursuit	48
Pathfinder	49
Undeniable End of Being	50
Broken Flowers	51
Dead Lovers	52
Empty	53
Fated	54

No Place To Run	55
Castles of Flesh	56
Mistress	58
Habit of Habits	59
Puzzles and Possibilities	62
Rocky Path of Life	64
Untitled	66
Thoughts	67
Untitled	68
Untitled	69
Choose	70
Where The Mountains Touch The Sky	71
Dream Chaser	72
Etched On Glass	73
Forest of Weeds	74
In The Dark Recesses Of Our Souls	75
Key Keeper	76
Love Lost	77
Memories Of Her	78
The Burning	79
Thoughts of Her	80
About The Author	81

INTRODUCTION

Just a minor note to those who might be interested in reading the poetical ramblings of a fellow passenger on earth...

My poetry focuses mostly on nature and the human condition.

TO THE READER...

Words, like paint, flow forth from the Poet's brush, and paint a canvas of ideas, memories, losses and loves. The years, cryptically etched on woven fibers, bleed our blood, breathe our breath, weep our tears and imbibe our ecstasies. The heights of human sublimity and the depths of our follies are exposed, the pride and the shame have leaked from the veins of humanity; black stains on white linen. Our struggle through the labyrinth of reason, uncovered. Our search for diety strengthened and questioned. Poetry is a longsword, forged in the mind, of ink and thought, beat out on the anvil of suffering and quenched in the waters of pleasure, to be wielded by the master to create absolute beauty, but clumsily by the fool to bring forth dross.

Like wild rain beating out a cadence on our hearts, poetry dances across our soul, thrilling our passions to unseen summits, then dashing us onto the dark shores of despair. Crisp dark letters on the page, like soldiers lined up on a battlefield covered with snow, fight and struggle for the supremacy of ideas, but in the end they are just words, and do not think for us and cannot act for us, we must own that, and interpret these echoes from the past, these weeds and flowers from the present and choose our future.

THE SEARCH

Eager yellow puppies
Tumble over themselves
Seeking their mother's breast.
Like a babbling brook
Scrambling over the rocks
Searching for the sea.

CLOUDS UPON THE GLEN

Crown of the firmaments
Nature's fragile breath
Graceful in your dance
Awesome in your wrath.
How did you come to sit
Upon the gables high?
Placed by god or angel
Where rainbows go to die?
Most days your count'nance fair
Is borne cross country side
To fill all men with joy
Who look upon your face.
Solace in you is found
Where ere your path is laid
Cooler the summer breeze
Under your skirts are found.
From the rafters of the world
Hung with purposed care
Expansive is your view
Unfettered is your path.
Elusive and ethereal
You chase across the sky
Whimsy is your play mate
The tempest is your guide.
Other times most pouty
A child with tantrum bound
Baleful beauty unleashed
Resplendent glory found.
Dark you climb the skies
Dark you smother the land
Dark I see your face
Dark are your demands.

I feel the tension mount
Earth seems to hold its breath
Quiet on the edge of storm
Portent is your name.
Fury in your bowels is formed
Rage against a wrong unseen
A Spartans ire is unleashed
As Justice blinds the sky.
Sword of light unsheathed
Brilliant against the night
Striking at the heart of dark
Blindly seeking the foe.
Follows the fiercest sound
Erupts the cry, of true love lost
Pain and sorrow embodied
The cry of Want unbridled.
Justice unwraps injustice
A soulful sound that pounds
And shakes the gates of heavn'
Demanding to be heard.
You rip the sky asunder
While the stage is yours
But soon your rage abates
Like coals that slowly die.
The heather sighs sweet relief

As the tempest slows your roll
Once more you billow peacefully
As angst melts into calm.
The breath of life renewed
Now follows in your wake
Smell of fresh tomorrows
Distill upon the land.
The suns last rays are filtered
Through your lacy hem
As rouge glows in your cheeks

AARON ZUFELT

>I bid to you farewell.
>Now comes refreshing night
>Slowly creeping o'er the hills
>To tuck you into bed
>To sleep, perchance to dream.

TAMER OF THE UNIVERSE

Earth...
A blue orb cloaked in black velvet,
A beauty in a dark galaxy,
A rock of strength,
Dominated and domesticated,
Tamed by the Human Race!
Man, raised above all others
On a pedestal of gold
Crafted by his own hand,
Has tamed the essence of fire,
Captured its spirit
And placed it in a box!
The mighty oceans,
Plowed to a fury
Below the bows of many ships,
Kneels before man!
Radio waves, though invisible,
Have been taught to bend
To the will of the Master!
Technology itself, molded
In the hands of the artist,
Does nothing more
Than obey its possessor!
Even Man himself had not escaped.
Battles fought, Nations conquered,
Villages raped; even Man is tamed!
Man has walked the earth...
He has walked the moon...
He has trapped the stars on shiny paper.
Tamer of beast and bird.
Man walks alone.
No mountain unconquered.

AARON ZUFELT

No plain unplowed.
Man, tamer of the universe!
But the tongue can no man tame.

LUNA

The moon, like a ship at sea
With its white sails raised
Skirts across an ocean of skies.
Oh to weigh anchor with that great vessel
To travel with Orion
And converse with Cassiopeia.

WORN OLD MEN

Worn and cracked and gray
Stands the old man on the street
Like a picket in a rickety fence.
Stands the pickets on the fence
Twisted and bowed and worn,
Like a group of old men gathered
Eager to speak of better days.

EBB

The ebb and the flow of my heart
Seems to rise and withdraw
With your presence or your absence,
And like a wooden vessel
Trapped by the leaving of the tide
I too flounder without you by my side.

LARKING

Lyrics of the lark, tumble through the air
Without care for time, neither weary with care
Sings she in the glade, notes like red ripe fruit
Full of sweetness bursting, ready to give joy
To every lost soul, who's heart dares to pause
In their weary path, and lend a weary ear.

WOVEN

We are woven of the dust
That neath our feet is trod
And by some miracle wrought
We are the sons of God

WISTFUL

How slender the wind finds the branches
That slumber on the trees now dormant.
Some straight and elegant, others gnarled,
And twisted, not unlike old Scrooge's soul.
Slowly they sway, raking at the wind,
A dance, wind and branch, as old as time.
Silence, and you might hear a lonely call
Of haunted voices drawn thin with age.
Mournful, yet full of wistful beauty
Softly caressing your weary soul.
Their sound floats softly on the breeze
Stirring thoughts of restless romantics
Who pause and listen not with ear alone.

UNOPENED BOOKS

It must be a burden heavy
You call yourself to bear
To be the judge of others
By the way they act or look.
And upon these poor souls levy
Your approbations and your fears
To know the end of the story
Without ever opening the book.
From afar in your finery you mock
And downcast your eyes as you pass
What awful creatures to you they are
As they linger in some dark nook.
You turn from those who seek your help
And draw from heaven a tear
At times to ease a guilty mind
A few bills your hands may brook.
Cast from heaven they must be
But pressing forward you soon forget
And by giving, feel the better person
Alas, their dignity you have took.

TOMORROW

Tomorrow is the hope of those who live unhappily today
Yesterday is the regret of those who don't look forward
Today is the iron, in the forge of our will, ready to be molded
Happiness is shaped on the anvil of our noble desires
Too often we blame fate, for the loathsome paths our feet wend
In truth, the fates watch as shadows, in dark somber chambers
Where we are the cruel jailers of our own lost happiness
The soul yearns to breathe freedoms crisp awakening call
To wander pathways lost like an unread book upon the shelf
Happiness distills upon the soul who lives in the limitless now
For yesterdays are fading and tomorrows are not written
Drink the now, like cool refreshing waters to your parched soul
Yesterday is always behind you, but always built by the now
Tomorrow we never touch, can be built beautifully in the now
To never know regret, build nobly, in the moment you are in
And just as yesterday's cannot but mimic what we play today
Existing as a trail of tears or smiles woven in the soul's tapestry
Tomorrows cannot blindly offer up paths, either of dirt or stone
Where forethought in the now did not weed, or lay down pavers
We, in the now, control who we were in our yesterdays
We, in the now, control what our tomorrows have to offer
Do not allow your tomorrows to be left to hollow hoping
Do not hope tomorrow you are smarter, braver, kinder...
Live in the now, study to be smarter, stand up to be braver,
Hold out a hand now, to be kinder, and slowly you will find
Tomorrows dim and unknown trails turning to golden pathways
While your yesterday's hold fewer and fewer regrets
Of things done, not done, by someone who only hopes
They can one day find happiness in tomorrow without
Striving, without searching, without seizing the day, now!

THE FALLEN

If love were true at all
Why then do angels fall
Is not an angel but a child
Full born of mighty god
How then like leaves are they
That wend a lower path
But at the end of day
Does not the mighty tree
Love not less mightily
The ones below as not

GILDED LILIES

The frog on gilded lily seeks
To hold more than he has.
Looking in the mirror below
He spies the better fellow
And jumping seeks to feel
His em'rald skin awaken
To the pleasure promised
By the devil in the mirror.
Now he glides in ecstasy
His former self a memory.
I too have jumped from lily pads
In willing indiscretion
Where in desire called.

OF DEVILS AND GODS

If you take an 'o' from good
And give it a tail straight up
Evil soon becomes the devil
And good becomes a god

good
  go d   o
           d   evil
    god   devil

LOST VIRTUE

Much like a rusty axe cannot teach
Muscle, the pain of long hard labor,
Dusty scriptures upon the shelf
Cannot unread, undone, bestow virtue.
Muscle once earned can be lost
When the memory of hickory is forgot.

OF TIDES AND TOWERS

Sandcastles in the sky
Playthings of the gods
Built by unseen hands
Toppled by unseen tides.
You strive to build anew
Soft against an ocean blue
These white sands full of mirth
Bubbling high above the earth.
Seagulls dot your image
Scavengers of the sky
Like graceful crabs that float
Frolicking on the breeze.
Your life spent on currents veiled
Ebb and flow of living breath
The push and pull eternal
Of zephyrs hidden touch.
Your towers reach for glory
Forever falling short
Tears you shed at failure
As you vanish in the waves.
You always bring us joy
We few who pause in step
View raised to a lofty beach
Like you to heaven we reach.

SUMMER

Summer is spent
Like an empty cartridge
In an old carbine
And like Achilles arrow flown
Can never be recalled
By any power known

EYES

Azure raindrops fall quietly
Red on roses blooms noisily
Echoes darken in the distance.

Truth is found in the eyes.
Heartache speaks without words
Etched upon the oracle of your heart.

Wise men weep.
Infants cry.
Night descends without darkness
Deepening the sorrow
Observed across two souls
Who struggle to understand.

To the hale and hearty
On the battlefield

The spoils of victory go.
Here in the minds' domain
Everyone feels the pain.

Silently the soul dies
Outraged at the injustices
Unleashed upon the world.
Lies, unspoken, still wound.

HER FACE

Light full upon her face
She smiles with angel grace
Mighty as an ocean storm
Meek as a gentle rain
She stirs a god in me
Where once a devil stood
Her eyes like emeralds shine
Her voice as sweet as wine
Her siren call I heed
And from the dust I rise
Free of this mortal coil
I saw the face of god

MY ANCIENT PICTOGRAPHS

Running through the house barefooted,
For making messes she's quite well suited.
With grit and grime and more to share,
She runs rampant with disheveled hair.
Leaving dirty handprints on each wall,
Then flirtingly flees trying not to fall.
Like pictographs of some long forgotten days,
Such are the handprints which she lays.
Now these are gone and no longer remain,
As time has ticked out its old refrain.
Those familiar echoes are now but shadows,
And my soul strives to follow where she goes.
But time may thrash and throw around,
And destroy all that to which it's bound.
Its power shall not erase nor tear apart,
These handprints gently etched upon my heart.

A CHILD CRIES (OKLAHOMA BOMBING)

Fear of loneliness
Fear of the unknown
Sitting half bathed in the shadows
A child cries.
Not old enough to whisper 'Mother'
Yet old enough to understand 'Mother'
Wide eyes and bright tears
A child cries.
Terrible noises
Fear, Uncertainty
Desperately the child extends her arms
Pleading for comfort.
More terrible noises.
Darkness.
Silence.
Jesus wept.

ADDED UPON

I look upon life's highest spire,
   To the place I have long desired.
This valley in which I dwell,
   Seems lowly, full of hell.
To see what I could be,
   But knowing what I am.
At the tools of life I look,
   These gifts of God I have forsook.
Grandly I could have built,
   But here I stand full of guilt.
To see what I could be,
   But knowing what I am.
Other men have climbed so high,
   I'd sell my soul for wings to fly.
But through God's wisdom I must crawl,
   So as not to think I know it all.

SLEEP FALLS ON THE MOUNTAIN

Snow, slowly drapes across
The mountains craggy mane
Like smooth white linen thrown
On furniture antique.
Autumnal mountain sounds
Quiet under winter's white
Slumber and wait for younger days
Sleeping soundly like a bear.
The snow itself falls sleepily
A lullaby to the living unsung
Sweet and slow and peaceful
Like a mother rocks a child.
The pines grow slowly dim
Through the curtain of snow
Assuming a ghostly white
Summoned to another realm.
Dream, mountains, dream
As you slumber neath the white
Dream of fields of columbines
Spangled on the verge,
Bluebells and marigolds
Playing with the wind untamed
And rivers running clear
Like soft music from a flute.
Soon to your dreams will come
Stags upon the shadowed glade
Proud statues in a garden
To ease a restless sleep.
Make a pillow of the clouds
And pull the blankets tight
Cold winter soon will wane
Like memories grown old.

SUM OF LIFE

I stare into this fire
These logs that keep me warm
And see our human lives
Full written start to end.
When born, the fire is lit
Slowly enough it starts
Creeping, learning...growing
Venturing not afar.
Soon if feels its power
And blazes with fervid heat
As long as there is fuel
It burns most greedily.
Once past the fiery blaze
Now rules the glowing coals
Wisely conserving their fuel
Yet slowly they too dwindle,
And flicker their last red
Growing colder by degrees
In the end but ashes dark
To mark where once it lived.

LIFE'S ABACUS

A fiery bead on a cosmic abacus, dividing now from was,
Sorting one day from the next, one act from the last.
Summing our existence, without care without pause,
It sifts our yesterdays and tallies our tomorrows.
The mightiest mathematician alone gives it cause,
Plots it's coarse true, plowing through the eternal;
Order, it's charge, a mighty cog in a clockwork universe.
This Phoenix births all creation, lives untold awaken
We see the gardener gently sowing order and beauty,
Yet fail to see thorny scars upon his hands and wrists,
Hard works history firmly etched upon his mortal flesh.
This striving is where the mortal touches the eternal,
Shall we chain it with ambition and blackened avarice?
Shall we dull its glory with pride, gluttony and fear?
Shall we wound it eternally and strive not to heal
The wound that weeps the vigor of life from the soul?
No, this is folly, man mars not the beauty of that sphere,
Yet such we do to our better angels, bind their wings
Break their spirit, forced to graze on the bitter dust.
The beauty of our souls undone by ill placed blight.
Blot out the soul of the sun, a flower dies somewhere,
Darken the soul of man, innocence dies somewhere.
Weary is the existence loaded with chains that pull,
Chains we choose wrapped so tight we can't breathe
Drag our souls to the ground and crush without care.
Why do we wound our souls, why do we pick at scabs?
We comprehend beauty around us, are loathe to mar it,
Yet this creation of beauty we are, we fear not to mar.
If you remove but one from a dozen, it ceases to be,
How can beauty remain if you make it less than it is?

LIFE...

Trees giggle with the wind
It's caress, warm laughter.
Winters long grip grown weak
Tired of her cold work
She fades now, as a specter
Before lengthening days
Who shed no tears for her.
Begins the tireless work
Seeds breaching warm soil
Fawns struggling to stand
Leaves erupting in silence
Life once again conquers
Though the outlook is bleak.
Green leaves will turn to black
The stag falls prey to death
Plants wither where they grew
The cycle of life, of death
Repeats without weariness.
The sun rises, the sun sets
The seasons roll tireless
Incapable of rest
A river of time flowing
Searching for tomorrow.
Today, sacrificed on the altar
In hopes of better days.
Let nature be our guide
Her struggle never ceasing.
Decay will always come
His black hand touches all
Slowly fading beauty
All things to ash it turns.
Yet true death only comes
To those who don't fight back.

LARKING

Lyrics of the lark, tumble through the air
Without care for time, neither weary with care
Sings she in the glade, notes like red ripe fruit
Full of sweetness bursting, ready to give joy
To each and every soul, daring their heart to pause
In their weary path, and lend a weary ear.

FROM THE DEAD NEW LIFE

All things wintery soon wane
Like sin pressed by religion
She weakens with the spring.

Her grip once icy cold
Around my bony frame
Now slackens with the sun.

The golden globe renewed
Spring rises strong once more
Winters prize to her denied.

Soil moist from winters fare
Dead stalks from falls excess
Warm breeze, a promise of life.

Sphere of creation turns
And from the dead new life
And from the dead new hope.

Feel the vigor rising
Where once did vapid lie
The seeds of humankind.

A smile to warm the heart
A kind word to heal the soul
And flowers blossom in the mind.

As surely as seeds bloom
With warmth and water too
So too a kinder soul
Is born in gentleness.

TANGLED LEAVES

Leaves lie tangled on the ground
Like shavings from a sculptor
Casting off the excess bulk
In search of hidden beauty within.
Winter too, removes the unwanted
In search of other beauty lost
A hidden, new palette to show
With strokes, not quite so bold
Muted, still alive, still vibrant
Relevant without trappings.
Perhaps not as was Solomon
But like Job, once stripped of all
To give eyesight to look beyond
And still see the master's hand.

THE WEIGHT OF WINTERS

The weight of winters dreary
Lies heavy on my soul.
No more the call of birds
Fall gaily from the branch
Silenced and cold are they
Dare, I say, as a coffin
Wherein no sound escapes.
No more the sound of children
Laughing in the park
Silenced too soon are they
Like a bell that hangs un-rung.
Winter is a teacher stern
Whose frigid glance soon cools
The happiness of earthly men
And wrings the days of joy.
Dull are the clouds and sky
Like wash-water used too much.
No color allowed by the miser
So hope has not on what to kindle.
Winter is full of waiting turned cold
Like waiting for a lover lost
You know will not return.
Dried leaves hang spent on branch
Where once they lived have died.
Withered and tired, they also lie
Near the foot of their proud author
Like so many crumpled papers
Where bad poems lay a dying.
Such is the weight upon my soul.
Humanity also frigid turns
Pushing, shoving, no color
No love on a neighbor lost.

AARON ZUFELT

All content to allow cold hate
To freeze all human relation.
The slow stream of humanity
Freezes over, like creek water
Too weak to fight the biting ice.

RAINDROP ON THE BACK PORCH RAILING

Its feeble mass
Ill enabled gravity
To gain its small reward.
Hung suspended
Like a spider waiting
Does it contemplate
Space or elusive time?
Does it strive to descend
To the unknown below?
Does it not curse the fate
Of its journey upheld?
Lonely it must be waiting
Like water crystals frozen
Anticipating the caress
Of springs warming breath.
Once more the rain begins
Coolly slicing at the skies.
Helped by its own kind
It pushes on the boundaries
Of what It had become
And glides wetly into the beyond.

FOREST PINE: PART ONE

Slowly a second death
Falls upon a proud prince
Of mother nature's realm.

This child of the sun
Grown old from the passing
Of many winters' grasps.

Let fall his last fine robes
Stripped of earthly pride
Full naked in the moon.

Now he stands in silence
As seasons come and go
A ghost of better times.

Though dead he seems alive
Still shapely in the sky
Still pleasing to the eye.

Slow failing in his form
His life spent striving up
Gives up the lofty heights.

At last he comes to rest
No longer in the fray
Brought low by slow decay.

No dancing with the wind
No deep embrace with earth
No brotherhood with life.

Now laying he can rest
The earth in full embrace
New foliage for a cloak.

Faded his long shadow
Prostrate his erect form
No more his memory.

FOREST PINE: PART TWO

Where stood once the prince
Now shyly takes the stage
New life from old retold.

From his moldy decay
Memory anew is born
Striving for lofty heights.

Delicate as fresh dew
Soft as a gentle wind
hope of tomorrow glows.

Warm falls heavens light
Azure fields siren call
Motive power obeys.

Moist strength falls quiet
Light caress of Gilead
Promise of life renewed.

Raiment new without cost
Royalties true color
Tears of Onuphrius.

Roots find glory in diving
Vigor pulses within
Truly life triumphs.

Dancing with the wind
Deep embrace with earth
A brotherhood with life.

Youth that teems with grace
Wonders yet to know
Life is new and bold.

Days spent idle in the sun
Days fresh with busy joy
Days that never end.

New his regal shadow
New dawn of memories
New child of the sun.

GLIMPSES OF BULL TROUT LAKE

Pine trees dark against a night sky,
Masts of a ghostly fleet with tattered sails.
Stars bright against a darkened heaven,
Reflections of light on a wet onyx beach.
Owl, a lonely vigil of passing time,
A vessel at sea marking its weary passage.
Fire twisting around broken limbs,
Hands grasping yet never grabbing.
Smoke lifting gently from our altar,
Wraiths content to wander aimlessly.
Bats swimming through smoke after insects,
Spectral shadows giving chase in ether.
Gravel loud under my passing feet,
Gritty rhapsody in the nightly cacophony.
Bull Trout Lake sleeping calmly,
A mere puddle before the raging storm.
Hail and rain beating down from the sky,
Hammer on anvil, hammer on anvil.
Wind racing down mountains across the lake,
Passion coursing hotly in the blood.
Echoes rattle across the lake,
The future foretold by young and old.
Shooting stars bold across a star weary sky,
Memories recalled and quickly lost to time.

IN THE MIDDLE

Laman's pine less top, without cap it did shine,
Bobbing in Martin Lake, like the float on my line.
Always floating Bull Trout, in his kayak he perched.
Ever vigilant, it was for elusive trout that he searched.
Cooking his catch, was a flamboyant affair,
His succulent trout, always willing to share.
Helene would have won, if trophy there'd been,
She pulled in her limit, one more would be sin.
She'd stay in her small tent, till morning was past,
Yes to lunches, and dinners, but never breakfast.
At the fires she basked, and burned her mallows well done,
And the eyes of her trout fishes, she'd offer to all and one.
Gerald The Elder, author of five, retired quite early,
On the premise of work, though it seemed quite squirrelly.
Scrambler of eggs, and dutch oven extraordinaire,
We ate his tasty creations, with gusto and flair.
Hoods he propped up, to keep lazy rats honest,
His daughter to tryouts, he took as was promised.
Lee Ann was the hen, that ruled the tenth roost,
Leading her clutch, save one, she'd rather have noosed.
Bandages, brunches, snacks, and fine meals,
Her other half ran off, with her sweet set of wheels.
Peering out of her tent, one morning she searched,
It was but a dog, that noisily watered the earth.
Lee tried his old hand, at the rod and the reel,
Fisherman he was not, so gave up the whole deal.
He liked to play hearts, but would not shut up,
And made a mean roast, that made for good sup.
Along with his sister, there was something forgot,
Oh yeah, spaghetti and sauce, for the old dinner pot.
Gerald The Younger, most times tried to please,
To be rugged his cot, he did place under the trees.
But the threat of more rain, made him rightly quit,
And those cowboy boots, sure filled him with grit.
Row, row, row, his boat, gently cross the lake,
For to try and land, as many fish as he could take.
Joan made good use, of the shower we brought,

And readily sipped, each mornings hot chocolate.
She helped with the dishes, and did a fair bit of reading,
Through it all she did smile, and had her share of sleeping.
Sampling the trout fishes, she liked them quite well,
But would prefer Potter, and a good magic spell.
Nichole was quite good, and helped her mom lots,
And probably washed, her fair share of pots.
One time with her family, she raced back to camp,
But first ended up last, (and I'm getting writer's cramp).
She tore a hole in her sock, and the complaints we did hear,
She got to go home early, (she wanted internet I fear).
Neri the indelicate, with both frogs and farts,
Could stir up the whole camp, and not just parts.
He ate his dogs cold, no bun nor condiment,
He'd sure show his dad, what stubborn meant.
When it came to eating, not a soul could compare,
He ate the whole camp, and had room to spare.
McCloud could be found, in his hoodie most times,
And playing with Legos, on rocks and tall pines.
Cereal is a delicacy, he was once heard to say,
I'm' sure if he could, he would eat it all day.
Near to the fire, was his favorite spot,
Unless he was crawling, into dad's warm cot.
Aurora was a big help, when it came to cracking eggs,
She whipped them up nicely, few shells in the dregs.
Always walking barefoot, around camp she did go,
Leaning on a walking stick, ambling to and fro.
Down at the beach, lost a Lego person she did,
Hours of searching, finally found it well hid.
Jasmine always awoke, with incredible hair,
The envy of women, and others who care.
Slyly taking the camera, from the Maid of Orleans,
She took some quick selfies, or so it would seem.
Holding the toads, whenever she could,
Finding a prince, now that would be good.
Many times round camp, the idiot we played,
We had lots of fun, more days we'd have stayed.
The rain on the tents, as we listened at night,
The Old Willow Witch, who gave us a fright.
Visits from bog people, gnawing on digits,
Ghost and ghouls, that would turn you religious.

Round the campfire bright, rumors were spread,
Some bout the living, but mostly the dead.
We all made it home, you can most surely see,
Best fun to be had, is to camp with family.

THANK YOU CHILD

Youth is but forgotten secrets of the past
Memories of a time well spent
And forever sought after again.
The smell of burning wood
In grandfathers old iron stove,
The caress of cool grass
As you lie beneath the stars,
The grandeur of dreams
Never quite forgotten
Yet never quite attained.

It is in vain at night
That I try to recall youth.
The creak in the floor,
The flowers in the kitchen window,
Or that certain way the drapes
Would float lazily in a soft spring breeze.

It is in vain
That I clench my fists
And struggle against time
For that which I cannot keep.
Then I smile, for I cheated
And time had not won,
For these secrets are not forgotten
Just put away to be treasured
To guard against corruption.

I found the key to unlock these secrets;
It lies in the eyes of my own child,
It lies in her tiny hands,
And in the smile she so freely gives.

Thank you child.

SOUL FORGE

Restless nights sing of love
Two hearts that beat as one,
Raging in the endless night
Beating out an ageless song.
The forge glows eerie white
Strike while the steel is hot,
Hearts, souls, and minds
That intertwine, combine
A stronger alloy of two souls.

SOME REASON MORE

Is this our life to live
To stumble and to rise
To but stumble again?
Is this our life to live
A broken heart to mend
To but break again?
What is the point
Of thorns upon a rose
To prick the ones they love?
What is the point
Of wings upon a dove
To leave the ones they love?
Is there no more to life
Is there no more to love?
Just paint that never sticks
Always peeling from the soul,
you scrape and paint again
Again it shrinks and cracks.
My heart tires of this lot
And seeks some reason more.

RESTLESS THE NIGHT

The crescent moon slopes deeply
As delicious night falls suddenly
Surrounding budding flowers
In shadows cool pathway
Soft as a king's silken tapestry.
Then centaurs laugh again
Like new love and old wine.
Then Juliet weaves desires garland
Across crag and earthen mountainside
And Romeo wears and olive crown
And gives her a kingly flask
Of fallen stars found frozen
In aged trees last flowering
On distant shades of land.
Like shadows of old
He clings only to her.
Then they are gone
As the golden orb awakes
Full of hungry passion that drinks
Mist from the very air.
And they become again
The cypress and the oak.

THE PURSUIT

The moon chases the sun
As night chases the day,
Youth grasps at immortality
As fire grasps at smoke,
My heart pursues hers
As moths pursue the flame,
My soul seeks out hers
As rivers seek the sea.

PATHFINDER

A feeble mind is easy pray
To wickedness and sin
Left to its own device
Of seeking lower ground
Causes wanton chaos
Unbounded misery
Yet dam the mind up tight
Against licentious thought
The rivers of the mind
Will be a fount of strength
A refuge from the storm
Wherein the devil knocks

UNDENIABLE END OF BEING

Emphatically the mouse died
Like a pale leaf fluttering
Trying to unhinge itself
Captive of a brittle branch.
So too should we all meet fate
Wearying ourselves against
Destiny's last and fatal call.
Blowing the horn of Gondor
Searching for our brother true
Pining for a worthy captain
Seeking one to call our king.
Exhausting our final strengths
In one last show of glory great
Impervious to our mortal wounds
We will stand and cry mightily;
This clay you may asunder rend
This spirit remains forever free.
And from my blood will bloom
Virtue on tomorrow's rose
To stain my enemy's hands
And courage in the morning dew
To strengthen kindred souls
Who weary against the flesh
In search of higher reason
To consume the empty void
That would consume all men.

BROKEN FLOWERS

My heart swells with compassion
For the pain of my fellowman.
I cry at my ineffectual ability
To ease the suffering of a friend
Or my ineptitude to alleviate a stranger
Of the unseen burden they might bear.
But roughest of all on my tender being
Is a child in the blossoming spring of life
Broken, sad, hopelessly lost
Eyes forlorn, ageless against their youth
Beaten, hungry, without a friend.
In this world of superfluous wealth
The small and weak are forgotten
Trodden down and left behind
Like a small child at a piñata game
Left standing with nothing but shame
Feeling that they are at fault.
But the blame lies squarely on our shoulders
For we are their designing fates
And we must share their future.

DEAD LOVERS

These the moon did leave repulsive
And weak beneath its cool shine
Like rain without a summer garden
Or a forest, black from want of stormy spray.
No tongue nor shadow could foretell
The bitter dream of springs worshipping love
Torn apart like petals from a rose.

EMPTY

When empty bellies gnaw
Like wolves chewing on a bone
The keen edge of life is felt
Like a knife at the throat.
Deaths empty face floats
In visions beyond seeing
On a precipice one stands
Devoid of real intent.
Empty dreams gnaw also
Like acid slowly etching
Leaving life quite hollow
Fragile like a dried bone.

FATED

Thus our fate to meet
Was written in the stars
When they were wild and young
We are the essence of poetry
Written for all to see
Our lips like lovers lost
Now found to never part
Our eyes locked in embrace
Never to unwind

NO PLACE TO RUN

Something wicked
this way comes
And all I see is mirrors
Who is this man I see?
A burning in his heart
I turn, I run, I...
There he is again
Standing in my way
Will he never leave
Once more I turn to run
Once more he seeks me out
I weary of this chase
I weary of no escape
The flesh upon my bones
Grows tired of this game
To run and hide to but
Run and hide again
And then I see her there
Can I dare hope she too
Sees me on these shores
Of my endless torment
Can I dare hope she comes
To wipe my fevered brow
To show a better way
To carry my heavy heart
In her soft and gentle hands
To lay me in green pasture
Beside the now still water
To mend my brokenness
That I might be whole again
We might together be whole

CASTLES OF FLESH

My tears of sorrow fall dark
Upon the sands of time
To be slowly washed away
By the endless tides of life.
And the devil just laughs
As he plays with my soul
Like an angry hurricane
Beats with fury on a boat.
These sands upon the shore
They were not always so
Once proud stone of grand design
Grim in visage, pure in heart.
Worn thin by passing time
And beat of wind and rain,
Slowly brought to nothing
Ashes of a regal lineage.
What chance have I, have we
Against the might and main
Of humanities baser wants
We Children of Sisyphus.
If a rock born strong will bend
How then shall flesh bear up
I fear, like the Bard foretold
Like straw to fire in our blood.
Ask not for whom tolls the bell
If one man falls, fall we all
Like a child's castle of sand
Before the ignorant tide.
Fear not the dark you see
The dawn will always come
No man can hold it back
No deed can stay it's coarse.

And like the smell of rain
Brings promise of renewal
So too the light of dawn
Urges all creation on.

MISTRESS

Feel the fiery spray of the sea
Smell the salty water on the breeze
Hear the soft hum of heavens engines
Churning tireless against the shore
The bosom of the earth heaving
Forever restless against its bounds
Mistress to many a young seaman
Full spellbound from crib to tomb
A graveyard to others far from home
Who answered well her siren call
Tortured by native winds and rock
Caressed by silky smooth shores
Can you hear her softly calling
When you gaze upon her beauty
Hear me, go join your soul with hers
For she shall be a loyal lover who
Will leave not nor break your heart
But your soul is hers, she shares not
And when this life's end has come
Go to her, she will hold you still
Pity not those who have no love
Rest peaceful in her cold embrace

HABIT OF HABITS

In despair I tasted bitterness
For so it was decreed
All souls at times must taste
The bile which burns the world.

But as a sinking boat un-bailed
Must surely embrace cold death
So too those who do acquire
The bitter taste of loathsome ways.

Men who cling to errors paths
Are not unlike that boat
Who sinking, loses by degrees
The firmaments bright light.

Descending into a darkly pit
Ruin written on their bow
To a world of crushing woe
Dense with wooden husks.

These once of proud design
Who did one time permit
This habit of water leaking
Which proved to be their doom.

Youthful spirits too, grow warped
On a diet of worldly filth
Which corrodes their wooden souls
And cankers once fine prows.

All habits are living things,
Those that push us upwards
Or those that pull us down
Both know from whence they come.

For once these seeds are cast
Where ere the fount may be
Flowing from mount liberty
Or wasted lands most foul.

It matters not where in this world
Or how far your path may go
These habits are like salmon
Forever returning home
A primal urge to satisfy.

If you must taste bitterness
Linger not upon its taste
For as with our mortal clay
So our spirit half the same.
What is consumed you are.

Dress your habits and desires
In modesty's good taste,
Too many in rags are found
And dregs from gutter filth.

Perhaps if all could see them
These burdens we choose to bear
As easy as the clothes we wear
We would more careful be.

Yet hardest on our societies
Is nature's primal rule
Forged at creations door
Which states; like must breed like.

For weeds will not breed roses
Nor bread rise up from stone
That which you sow you reap
Indelibly is stamped
like commandments on our bones.

So where your habits drive you
Your children will most likely
As once did Mary's lambs
Follow where ever you may go.

PUZZLES AND POSSIBILITIES

Life is like a picture puzzle
As we slowly spend our days
Gently piecing truths together
Which all become much clearer
The closer we near the end.
Some pieces we try to force
Others fall neatly into place
There is only one sure truth
We will never see the whole
If we don't work at the parts.
Older hands become familiar
With the feel of these life tiles
And bored perhaps at times
At the monotonous pace of life
Or burdens under which we toil.
Forever searching for the One
Piece that fills a searing void
Both pain and happiness can
And will, linger for a lifetime
Fragmented pictures that we own.
While younger hands rejoice
At the newness of the game
To them, life is crisp and clean
A new puzzle box unwrapped
Infinite worlds of possibilities.
Just now emptied on the table
Unceremoniously spilled
Life's promises, gathered in a pile
Ecstasy written in their eyes
New discoveries on each hand.
Let them own their newfound joys
Revelations in clouds and flowers

Wonders in green grass and bugs
How water turns the dirt to mud
And kisses turn frowns to smiles.
For sorrows come too soon and oft
As life knocks the newness off
And we tend to lose some pieces
We were wrong to not hold close
Which drop and remain unfound.
Now our own life's portrait is
Not certain as the picture which
Is found upon the puzzle box
Each choice we make in life
Alters somewhat the final draft.
And all have darkened puzzle parts
Works which cannot be undone
Denial of one's darker frames
Hoping ignorance spawns bliss
Leaves you lesser than the whole.
For when the morning sun does shine
The daisy too does shadow cast
Yet from her this shade remove
And she is left with half a soul
For light exists despite the dark.
So every point of dark must have
A counterpoint of greater worth
Filled with beauty and reverent awe
Greater joys to mask our sorrows
Greater strength to carry faults.
And when we have laid our final piece
May God rest our weary souls
And pray those who are dear to us
Find solace for their own puzz'ling
In remembered moments shared.

ROCKY PATH OF LIFE

Tomorrows are not so dim
As to trade them all away
For cold dreams of what might be.
Seek a friend for they too know
Of life, rough as jagged rock
And endless days of lonely.

Sits alone a sentinel stone
Surrounded yet by other rocks
In a garden of crowded solitude.
The sun bakes him, does he cry?
Winter freezes him, is he hurt?
Does he see or feel or care that
His companion rocks nearby
Endure life the same as he?
If these rocks could talk or laugh
Their long days and weary nights
Away, perhaps their lot would be
A simpler course to wend awhile.

Worry not the rocks next door
Desire no concourse with thee
For once was pen and paper
Carried cross land and sea
And weeks to see it through.
Now you carry all your friends
Wherever your path may wend
Surely there is one who cares?

How many billion humans wrought
That weave a lonely path and die
Or Is it that we truly fear to live?
Do not think all pain is yours

That others have not ever felt
The hands of deaths despair,
Or souls stripped of vitality
Leached of all things human,
Like a desert waterhole which
Alkali has turned to venom
No longer a source of life.

No one is ever so alone
As to feel the need to quit.
Raise your courage but an ounce
Cast wide your glance around
Fear not to raise your feeble hand
This is by far the better part
And in receiving a little help
Might you also feel inclined
To seek those whose arm may flag.
For as the Poet once gave ken
"Know we more our fellow men?
Human suffering at our side,
Ah, like yours is undescried!
Us, unable to divine
Our companion's dying sign."

UNTITLED

Leaves lie crumpled
On the forest floor
Like socks once used
now just tossed aside
Left to rot like corpses
Whose essence now is free
To other pathways wend
And other toils attend

THOUGHTS

Some thoughts are like butterflies
Softly lighting upon our minds
Creating the smallest of sensations
Overwhelming our being with beauty
Too soon they flit away and are gone
Our senses unable to grasp their beauty
Our chance lost to study their complexity
So vainly the moment we try to rebuild

UNTITLED

I thought I heard my name
Called by a youthful voice
Maybe a young boy Rowan
But I woke to the cat meowing
And chuckled at the thought
That maybe the cat knew my name
But perhaps it was my dad
Just passed but two hours now
letting me know he was ok

UNTITLED

The massive weeping willow
Branches hanging to the ground
Slowly undulating in the wind
Looked like a woolly mammoth
Marching across a gusty steppe.

CHOOSE

I am a nail
That pierces
That clings
Timeless to your soul.
Others are the rain
That quench a thirst
Then dry away
And are no more.

WHERE THE MOUNTAINS TOUCH THE SKY

I see at times the night
Run wild in your eyes
And love falls like rain
Upon our naked souls
You have branded me
I am marked as yours
Is your love a tyrant?
If so, rule over me
Is your love the truth?
If so, never lie to me
We shall together build
With our common clay
A destiny made for two
Where eternity is ours
You shall be the sky
I the mountains high
Forever is our embrace
No mortal can erase

DREAM CHASER

Like a father who has come
To chase away a bad dream
The sun rises on my miserable being
And distills in my troubled heart
The clear hope of a new day.
But like a stealthy cat creeps
To pounce on mice unaware
Shadows of darkness once more
Fall upon my helpless self
As I drown in a sea of grief.
Hands raised I reach for Father
Shunning the shadows I struggle
To embrace the lemon sunlight
That seems to elude my grasp
And pray not to be left in the dark.
I cry tears of sorrow and pain
As the thoughts of loneliness
Press unbearably on my heart.
Truly a miserable creature am I
Endlessly looking for a new sunrise.

ETCHED ON GLASS

Frost slowly weaving
With ancient fingers
Cold webs that draw
Secrets of the world
On my window pane
Fractals of the soul
Traced on silicate
From histories skeins
A fine thread drawn
To connect us all
Like finest silken lace
This book of memories
Is all too quick to fade
With the suns first rays

FOREST OF WEEDS

Weed weed weed weed
Weed weed weed weed
Weed weed weed weed
Weed weed weed weed
Weed weed weed weed
Weed weed weed weed
Weed weed flower weed
Weed weed weed weed
Weed weed weed weed
Weed weed weed weed
Weed weed weed weed
Weed weed weed.....

IN THE DARK RECESSES OF OUR SOULS

Aye to have a devilish woman
Who could stoke her passion high
And not exceed the earthen hearth
But burn the more greedily
For that kindling which it owns
And not let the logs lay cold.
A ship that knew her course
And raised the sails full mast
Her prow, straight and true
Did the bidding of the hand
That lay upon the wheel.
An arrow straight and pure
To pierce the oaken heart
Of but one wooden man
And cleave to him
Like the red center of a target
And not sit fallow in the quiver.
But strike fast and sure
And calm the restless beast
That threatens to destroy.
For it is no sin therein
To allow the beast to roam
Within the boundaries of its home.

KEY KEEPER

Those keys that you carry
Tell what do they unlock
The near future yet untold?
A dream yet made full whole?
Or is it something deeper
Kept safe from other eyes
The keys a lock do guard
Wherein the darkness lies
That never should be free
And if meant to lock away
And meant to be forgot
Why do you keep them so?

LOVE LOST

This thing which we call time
Running through my mind
Like water through my hands
So are the hourglass sands.
The shadow of a woman
Haunts my every thought
What we could have been
What we could have had.
Time, running through my fingers
Her hair, running through my fingers
Her kiss upon my lips
Memories of her scent
It was all so long ago.
We were happy for awhile
No one can deny us that
But like a flower that fades
Loves winter brings sadness,
Brings pain.
So here I am alone again
Never to know love again
Will loves winter never end?
Will my smile always be pretend?
Why can't I let her go?
Lost, how can love be lost?
I still feel it in my heart
It's traced upon my soul
Her kiss upon my lips
Memories of her scent
The shadow of her still
Walks across my mind.

MEMORIES OF HER

I trace the contour of her lips
A constellation in my mind
Soft yet firm on my fingertips
Velvet pages of poems unwrit.
A glance from her I see her soul
A universe I long to know
Her eyes speak love and mend me whole
Wells unfathomed unknown by man.
I hold her body close to mine
Like the dark is held by the night
Her touch ignites passion sublime
This destiny manifest in flesh.
Tonight I look for what once was
Eyes lifted in my mind's heaven
Searching the dark for signs of her
Memories etched like stars at night.
They guide my every waking thought
They disturb my moments of peace
I cannot sleep they pierce my mind
Bright stars in my mind's galaxy.
No longer am I bound to her
Sadly free from her guiding light
At times my weak eyes seek her out
But memories have grown so thin
Like stars that slowly dim and die.

THE BURNING

The moon through the mist does trudge
Its trip as timeless as the ache
Which sleeps in my soul each day
As a drop yet to drip from its perch
I dare not disturb its fitful rest
This burden on my bosom kindled
Would flare as a flame on a candle
To burn the bearer of the match
And not soon enough smolder and cool
And wait to be woken from slumber again

THOUGHTS OF HER

When I write, I write of her
When I speak, I speak of her
Maybe she was but a dream
Another vision of my mind.
Healing flows from her soul
Sealing up my old wounds
That never I could believe
Held the hope of healing.
Then sings my tired heart
Of blossoms on the tree
Blossoms that never die.
Then sings my tired soul
Of better days gone by
Days that never end.

ABOUT THE AUTHOR

Aaron Lee Zufelt

Aaron grew up in the mountain states of Utah and Colorado. Soon after marrying, Aaron and his family moved to Alaska and lived there for eight years. From Alaska, Aaron and his family trekked back down to the lower states and ended up in Idaho, where they still reside today.

Aaron has three wonderful children that have brought him countless joys. His first child was born in Colorado, his second child was born in Alaska and his third child was born in Idaho.

Like many children, Aaron grew to love reading at an early age, and remained an avid reader, growing up on a diet of westerns and science fiction. Later in life he added philosophy to his list of interests. His favorite authors include Jules Verne, Mark Twain, Louis Lamour, Plato and John Ruskin.

Aaron fancies himself a handyman and there are too many projects around the house half done. He enjoys gardening, anything scientific and also camping. Aaron tends to whistle when he's happy and does a good impersonation of a meadow lark. The household chores he prefers are vacuuming and laundry or anything that doesn't involve washing dishes.

Made in the USA
Columbia, SC
12 November 2021